S0-AJM-080

Women's Guide to Self-Defense

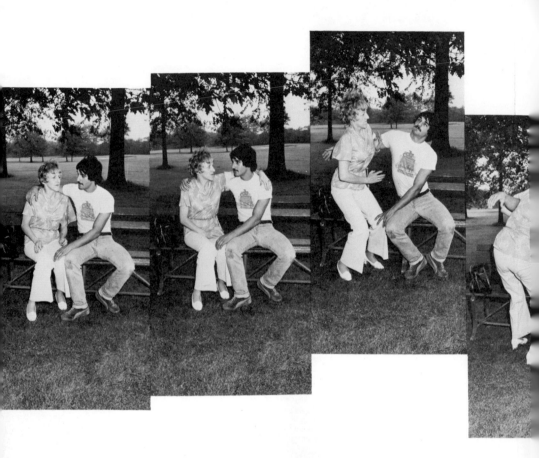

Michael DePasquale Jr.

Women's Guide to Self-Defense

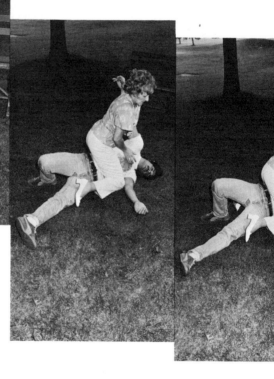

 CORNERSTONE LIBRARY • NEW YORK

This book is dedicated to my wonderful grandmother, Giovanna DeLuise, to my encouraging parents, and to all the women who are finally realizing it's time to stand up and strike back.

Copyright © 1980 by Michael DePasquale Jr.
All rights reserved
including the right of reproduction
in whole or in part in any form

Published by Cornerstone Library, Inc.
A Simon & Schuster Subsidiary of
Gulf & Western Corporation
Simon & Schuster Building
1230 Avenue of the Americas
New York, New York 10020

Designed by Irving Perkins/Eliot Kimble
Manufactured in the United States of America
10 9 8 7 6 5 4 3 2 1

"Cornerstone Library" and the cube design
are registered trademarks of Cornerstone
Library, Inc., a Simon & Schuster
Subsidiary of Gulf & Western Corporation.

Library of Congress Cataloging in Publication Data

DePasquale, Michael.
    Women's guide to self-defense.

    1. Self-defense for women. I. Title.
GV1111.5.D47   796.8'1   77-25009

ISBN 0-346-12455-7

I would first like to thank the individuals who are pictured on the following pages: Mario Buonomo, Josephine DePasquale, Lisa Stemplinger, Vinnie DePaola, Todd Knapp, Asa Katsorons, Olga Michelsen, and Gaetano C. Azzolini.

A special thanks is due to Gary Golembiewski, Rose Keleshian, Charlene Bass, Barbara Nasuto, and Between the Lens Studios for their pictures. Also to Ed Gavin and Charles Myers and the people at Simon & Schuster who made this book possible.

Hazel Spicer, Diane Meyer, Dawn Besemer, and my Mom and Dad deserve a very special thanks for their great encouragement.

Contents

Preface

Rape is the only violent crime that continues to increase. According to FBI statistics, reported rape has more than doubled—from 27,620 in 1967 to 56,730 in 1976. Many attribute the increase to women being more willing to report the crime. Others attribute it to society being more violent. Both factors probably influence such a large increase.

There is no typical rape victim, but most are young. In fact, over half are under twenty-one years old. She can be beautiful or unattractive, rich or poor, any color, creed, race, or size; rape can happen to any woman, anywhere, at any time.

Just as there is no typical rape victim, there is no typical rapist. Several studies have defined the rapist as the most normal of criminals—the most like the man on the street. According to statistics, if you are raped, chances are the rapist is someone you know, who lives nearby and planned the attack well in advance. More than half the time you'll be raped in your own home.

If he checks the listing on the mailbox or doorbell, "Jane Doe" informs him that there's a woman living alone. Windows and locks can be checked within a matter of seconds. One day's observation can let him know your routine, what time you leave and return, where you walk, how long it takes you to enter your building, whether you let others in when you enter, whether you lock the door when you leave for just a few minutes (to get the mail, walk the dog, or put in laundry), and most importantly, who else is around.

Rape is a crime that affects all women. Every time one of us is raped, each of us becomes slightly more afraid for ourselves, our children, mothers, grandmothers, sisters, and friends. We fear being alone, traveling late at night, using public transportation, and smiling as we walk. We spend money to take cabs, to live in safe neighborhoods, and to secure our homes with extra locks, window bars, and burglar alarms. We use up much of our mental energy wondering: What would I do if it happened to me or to someone I love?

Women are tired of accepting fear as a way of life. Consequently, we have become outraged. Outraged that since childhood we've been trained to be victims. Outraged that we've been defined as "naturally" passive, childlike, and vulnerable while men are defined as "naturally" aggressive, brutal, and uncontrollable. Outraged that we've never been taught to fight, to be assertive, to use our natural strengths and abilities, and to win. It is through this sense of outrage that we have come together, forming such programs as Women Against Rape and changing the institutions in which we work and in which we are consumers to respond to our needs.

I am involved in two such programs. I am a social worker in the Community Medicine Department at St. Vincent's Hospital and Medical Center in New York, where I coordinate the Rape Crisis Program. In this program, trained volunteer counselors living within a ten-minute radius of the hospital are on call once a month in their own homes. If a rape victim is brought into the emergency room, the counselor is called in to stay with the victim through the entire emergency room process. The counselors act as advocates for rape victims and their loved ones. At St. Vincent's I conduct ongoing training programs for both volunteer and professional staff, work with police, and collaborate with hospital staff to insure sensitive treatment of sexual assault victims brought to the hospital. We see approximately 250 sexual assault victims yearly.

I am also a member of New York Women Against Rape. NYWAR is a hotline and rape crisis center in Manhattan. At NYWAR I am a counselor on the hotline, which receives monthly approximately 125 calls from victims of sexual assault and 200 additional calls from women concerned with the problem of rape and what they can do about it.

The question most commonly asked is: Can't women do something to prevent rape? There is no one answer to that question. There is no perfect method that women can use to prevent rape. There are, however, preventive measures we can take.

First and foremost, we must accept and be aware that it *can* happen to any one of us. In fact, once we begin talking about rape with other women, we quickly learn that we have friends and relatives who have been raped and have never told us out of shame or fear of our reactions.

Once you are aware that it *can* happen, it is important to think about what you would do if you were attacked. Do you know how to defend yourself? Can you run in the clothing you usually wear? High-heeled shoes may look nice, but they are extremely difficult to run in. Where can you go for help if you're in danger? What stores are open late in your neighborhood? Where are the police phone boxes?

Think about your usual routine. Do you walk with confidence and alertness when you walk alone? Do you usually have your keys ready or do you fumble through your bag when you get to the door? Do you ever let others in even if you don't know them? Do you ever leave your door unlocked? Do you automatically open the door when you hear a knock or the doorbell? How is your name listed on the doorbell, mailbox, in the phone directory? Does it advertise the fact that you live alone?

How do you usually relate to men? Do you trust good-looking men? Older men? Younger men? Men who offer you help? With the groceries, for example? Men who are smooth talkers? Men who buy you a drink? A gift? Dinner? Men who are friends of friends? Or who offer to take you home? Or simply any man who doesn't look like a rapist?

What do you do when another woman is being hassled on the street, on a bus, or on a subway? Do you offer help? Pretend not to notice? Call the police? Become frightened? Or thank heaven that it's not you he's bothering?

How safe is your home? Do you have strong locks on doors and windows? Do you check them regularly? Do you have well-lighted hallways and doorways? Do you have a peephole or a safety chain? Do you always use it? Before allowing a serviceman into your home, do you check his identification?

These are just some of the factors you must think about to protect yourself against rape, or against any other crime. But what happens if a woman is attacked? What should she do to get out alive? Again, there is no pat answer. What follows is a profile of a rape situation. It was developed by New York Women Against Rape with the help of the Sex Crimes Analysis Unit of the New York City Police Department as a guide to help women prevent rape, and, if they can't prevent it, to get out of the situation alive and with the least amount of injury possible.

Of all the countermeasures mentioned, the most important is: Follow your instincts. I can't tell you how many times women I've counseled have said, "I felt something was wrong, but I couldn't put my finger on it, it was just a feeling I had. I thought I was getting paranoid." Or they worry about being nice: "I didn't want to let him in the building, but I just couldn't slam the door in his face."

Another critically important thing to remember is: Be suspicious.

Rape Alert: Countermeasures

1. TARGET SELECTION. Who will be the victim?

Factors of vulnerability	Countermeasures
Isolation.	Avoid isolated areas.
Accessibility.	Don't allow anyone to invade your space— don't be accessible.
Avenue of escape and minimum likelihood of interruption.	Stay with others.
Poor lighting.	Stay in well-lighted areas.
Weakness—physical and/or mental in-capacity.	Protect the vulnerable— don't leave them alone.

2. TESTING STAGE. Can the victim be intimidated or conned? Is the victim in need?

Factors of intimidation or connability	Countermeasures
Getting in close proximity.	Keep your distance.
Following.	Look like you belong.
Grabbing.	Be alert.
Asking for directions, change, etc.	Don't worry about being rude.
Flattery.	Don't give out info about yourself.
Promises of services or answering need.	Be suspicious— check out his qualifications.

3. THREAT STAGE. Can the victim be controlled?

Factors of control	Countermeasures
Attacker makes his demands known.	Follow your instincts.
Victim is usually threatened with death or bodily harm.	Check out how you match up physically and psychologically.
Victim may be physically injured.	Can you fight back? Run?
	Try to talk him out of it, buy time, and calm him down.

4. TRANSACTION OF SEX. Intercourse, sodomy, etc.

Factors	Countermeasures
Sometimes accompanied by additional threats, verbal abuse.	Endure it.
Attacker may give info about himself.	Do what it takes to stay alive.

5. TERMINATION STAGE. How the rapist makes his departure.

Factors	Countermeasures
Final statement—may be additional threat, order, apology, or bargain.	Do what you're told— it's safest.
May leave on foot, in car, run, etc.	Don't try to follow him.
	Don't be conspicuous about getting info such as license number.
	When you're *sure* he's gone—get to a safe place.

Remember, It Was Not Your Fault.

I've heard more than once, "I can't understand it, he seemed so nice. It's as if he's a Jekyll-Hyde or something." Or, "He seemed legitimate, it never occurred to me to check his identification."

Often women ask me, If I'm careful and avoid potential rape situations, do I need to learn to defend myself? Unfortunately, rape situations are not always avoidable and both physical and mental alertness are necessary to avoid rape. Most women who actively and immediately resist an attack get away. The rapist expects a victim, not an opponent. Part of the problem is that we regularly hear about the thousands raped; we seldom hear about the thousands who've successfully resisted.

The following are quotes from rapists taken from "Rapists Speak for Themselves" in *The Politics of Rape: The Victim's Perspective* by Diana Russell (New York: Stein & Day, 1975). "Had she yelled or screamed or struggled, I would have split" (Jimmy, page 245). "When I released my grasp on her, she went for my eyes. I jumped back, but she got me right below my eyes and raked downward with her fingernails. It was extremely painful, and I put my hands to my face and felt blood. That took everything out of me, and she was able to run out of the room" (Roger, page 250). "I don't think I could have gone through with it if she'd screamed. I honestly believe that if an individual would have put up a heavy fight, I would have walked away from it" (Fred, page 255).

Rapists don't usually pick their victims at random. They seek out the women least likely to resist, those who look helpless, unsure of themselves, and easily intimidated. Often you can deter an attacker by exchanging that air of passivity and vulnerability for one of confidence, determination, and assertion. You also must prepare yourself to resist immediately and to be willing to injure your attacker. Stamping on an instep, poking eyes, and kneeing the groin all may seem distasteful, but they require little strength to be extremely effective.

This book can help you learn the techniques to develop the necessary skills to physically defend yourself. Once you've mastered these techniques, you will be emotionally ready to act immediately in an emergency situation. Your instinct will be to size up the situation, the assailant, and your own ability, and to act accordingly.

Flora Colao

1

Basic Techniques

Before a woman can defend herself adequately, she must learn and practice certain basic techniques—the building blocks of self-defense. As she masters these basic techniques and acquires new knowledge and skills, her awareness of her own mental and physical powers will also grow and she will develop the total coordination and muscle control she needs to defend herself with confidence.

If you are serious about learning to defend yourself, you will put as much effort and concentration into it as you can. I strongly recommend that you devote at least one hour a day to the practice of the basic stances, blocks, strikes, and falls. If you get involved in self-defense heavily enough, you will find within your mind and body the inner strength that can come only from dedicated practice. This inner force has been called *Ki* by the Japanese. The essence of this difficult concept lies in the idea that the strength of a person cannot be determined by physical strength alone. Both mind and body must be unified before true power can be achieved. From time to time we hear of people who perform amazing feats of strength in moments of great stress; for example, someone lifts a car to free another who is trapped. The only reason that person could lift the car was that the mind and body, which normally function separately, were instinctively unified. For the self-defense woman, *Ki* is a goal to strive for—the ability to unify her mind and body at will and thus tap fully her potential strength and energy.

Always warm up and stretch at the beginning of your practice session.

2 Don't tire yourself out; just do enough to get relaxed and loose. During your warm-up, in addition to traditional exercises, such as sit-ups, push-ups, leg stretches, and jumping jacks, you should practice the basic stances, especially the tension stance. This stance is similar to the horse rider's stance, except that your feet are placed in a slightly pigeon-toed position, gripping the floor. Tense your body and expel all the air from your lungs, slowly breathe in again and relax. Assume the other stances and practice moving from one to another. These should become familiar to you and you should feel natural in them, ready to move in attack or defense. Throughout your practice session, try to begin and end each movement from one of these stances so that you develop the habit of always being in a balanced position ready for a new movement in any direction. Go slowly and concentrate on accuracy; speed will follow.

Before we move on to the basic blocks, strikes, and falls, let us look for a moment at the importance of *Kiai* to your self-defense. In practical terms, *Kiai* is a loud shout that you should incorporate into all your practice exercises. If you are grabbed by an attacker, a loud, self-asserting yell will very probably instill your assailant with fright or shock; at the least, it should throw him momentarily off balance. *Kiai* is more, however, than a mere shock tactic. *Kiai* is both psychological and physiological effective. The expulsion of air through your lungs increases your strength. It is not enough just to yell; you must expel all the air from your throat and diaphragm. You should be able to feel all your muscles tighten at the moment of expulsion. Properly done, a *Kiai* will help you attain maximum strength at the same time it frightens your attacker.

Practice *Kiai* with all the basic movements—strikes, blocks, and falls. Do not be embarrassed; it may someday save your life.

You can begin your practice for self-defense alone, using a mirror, until you feel comfortable in your movements. Use the horse rider's stance as the starting point for blocks and hand strikes. (For kicks you will use the other three basic stances—the forward stance, cat stance, and side stance.) As you progress and gain confidence, find someone to be your partner; you can take turns assuming the attacker's role and practicing the basic defenses shown in this book.

Let us take a look at the positions of the hand that you will use for most of the strikes and grabs in your self-defense arsenal. The hands are one of the most important weapons you have. There are many different hand positions and strikes beyond the traditional fist punch. With the hand held flat, you can

Stances

TENSION STANCE
This stance is most commonly used when you are doing a tension exercise. Your feet are slightly pigeon-toed, bent, and gripping the floor.

SIDE STANCE
Place one of your feet on the side of the knee of the other leg, as you face toward the side of the bent leg. You are now ready to snap out a side kick to any part of your attacker's body.

HORSE RIDER'S STANCE
With your upper body crouched over, bend your knees and feet slightly. You should feel as though your legs are straddled across the back of a horse; hence this stance is called the horse rider's stance.

FORWARD STANCE

Place your feet about shoulder-width apart, at a forty-five degree angle to each other. Bend your forward leg, while keeping your back leg straight.

CAT STANCE

With one leg bent and facing toward your side, bend your other leg in front of you. The heel of your forward foot should be up and facing the side of your rear foot. The forward foot is now in a position to kick.

use the fingertips to thrust or you can chop with either edge of the hand—the
knife-edge or the inside knife-edge. The illustrations show the portions of
the hand used to deliver the blow. With the hand in a fist position, you can
strike with the knuckles straight on or with the backfist; you can strike down
or across with the hammerfist and reverse hammerfist. You can open the
fist partway and strike with the heel of the hand. A variation of this strike is
the palmhand strike, in which the hand is cupped. Finally, by opening the
cup into a claw, you are ready for a clawhand strike, usually aimed at the
eyes or the Adam's apple. As you practice these strikes in the mirror, go
slowly and concentrate on form and balance; speed and self-confidence
will follow.

When you begin to practice with a partner, you should spend a part of
each session working on your grabs. Grabs are used when your attacker's
hand has come to rest somewhere on your person. You can grab your
attacker's hand from either side with one or both hands; the object is to put
painful pressure on his wrist. With an outside wristlock, you turn the
attacker's hand so that his thumb rotates up, over, and away from his body
at the same time his wrist bends toward his forearm. Press with your thumb
or thumbs as hard as you can into the back of his hand. With an inside
wristlock, you turn the attacker's hand down, under, and back, at the same
time you put pressure on the wrist as before. The third basic grab is the
downward wristlock. Grab the attacker's hand with both of your own and
force the wrist back and down.

Kicks may be delivered with the ball or heel of your foot, with either side of
your foot, or with the instep. You may kick up or sideways, or you may punch
with your foot. You can use the side of a shoe or its heel to rake or scrape an
attacker if he has you from behind, and of course you can stamp down on
his instep.

In addition to the offensive movements, you should incorporate defensive
movements into each practice session. In the following pages you will see
demonstrated a dozen blocks and falls. You can practice these movements
alone, but you should use a partner as soon as possible. Again, begin slowly
and concentrate on balance and form. When you practice blocks, get used
to using them when moving forward and when falling back. If you are
attacked, you must always move forward if you see the strike coming in time
and backward when the strike is already moving quickly toward you. You
should move immediately from a block into a strike or a fall.

As you acquire self-confidence and ability, you should build into your

Strikes

FINGERTIP THRUST

KNIFE-EDGE STRIKE

INSIDE KNIFE—EDGE STRIKE

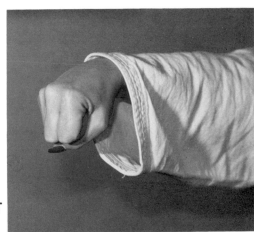

KNUCKLE FIST

BACKFIST

HAMMERFIST

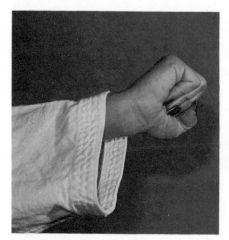

REVERSE HAMMERFIST

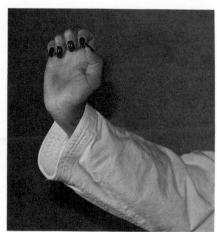

HEEL OF HAND STRIKE

PALMHAND STRIKE

CLAWHAND STRIKE

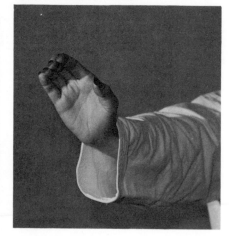

practice sessions the goal of a continuous series of movements. If you are attacked, you will not make a move and wait to see what happens; you must carry out a constant counterattack until you are out of danger. The final sets of illustrations in this chapter show you two continuous exercises. The series of strikes you will be practicing are done while the attacker has you in a bear hug—one from behind, one from the front. Practice each series first to the left side and then to the right. Do all the strikes in succession, slowly at first, then with moderate speed, and finally with full speed. You should begin, as you gain confidence, to develop a definite sense of where and how to strike and how much force to use.

Go on now to the strikes in chapter 2. In that chapter, I have focused on strikes and their target areas. As you gain self-confidence, you must also think about your attacker's vulnerability. In chapter 3, more attacks and counterattacks are illustrated. Work through these situations and then go on to devise counterattacks of your own. Finally, in chapter 4, you will learn how to use other weapons—ones that you will be likely to have with you—and incorporate them into your self-defense movements.

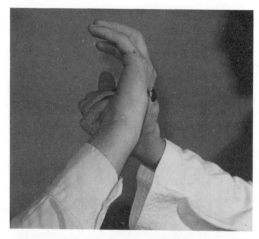

Grabs

**ONE-HAND OUTSIDE
WRISTLOCK**

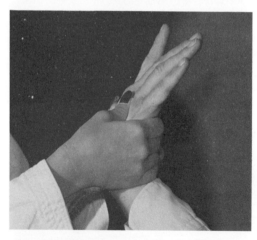

**TWO-HAND OUTSIDE
WRISTLOCK**

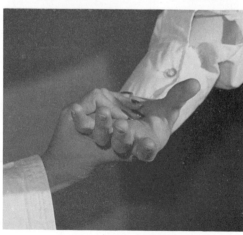

**ONE-HAND INSIDE
WRISTLOCK**

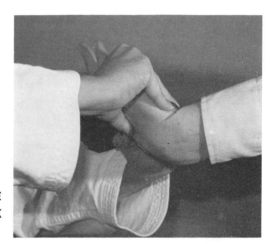

**TWO-HAND INSIDE
WRISTLOCK**

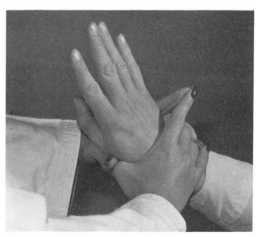

DOWNWARD WRISTLOCK

Blocks

HIGH BLOCK

In a counterclockwise motion, swing around and block a facial strike with your forearm. Your arm should always be bent at the elbow.

HIGH BLOCK WITH FIST

In a counterclockwise motion, swing around and block with your forearm while your hand is in a fist position. As you are blocking, the palm of your fist is turning so that it is facing your attacker. Your fist is always closed tightly.

INSIDE MIDDLE BLOCK

With your elbow staying down near your mid-section, your forearm comes around in front of you in a counterclockwise motion. Keeping your fist clenched tightly, your forearm will block your attacker's strike directly to the outside.

OUTSIDE MIDDLE BLOCK

As you step to the outside with your foot, or move into a cat stance position, your forearm comes out in front of you with your elbow bent. Now swing across the front of your body with the forearm and block your attacker's midsection strike.

SWEEPING LOWER BLOCK

As your attacker is punching to your groin or kicking you, come up across your body, with your elbow bent. Now drive it downward and swing across your body to block your attacker's strike.

CHICKENHEAD BLOCK WITH BACK OF WRIST

As your attacker punches to your face, squat down low and drive the back of your wrist directly up the middle of your body. Now guide your attacker's face punch directly upward past your face.

Falls

BACK BREAKFALL

1. With your feet apart, squat slightly down-ward with your hands in front of you.

2. Now kick out your feet and proceed to fall backward.

3. As you fall, keep your head up and look between your legs. Keep your arms straight out at your sides so that when you hit the ground they can absorb the shock of your body weight.

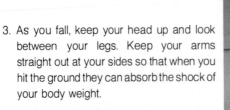

FORWARD BREAKFALL

1. Step forward with your right foot, preparing to put your right hand on the ground.

2. Now kick your left leg up toward the ceiling and push off your right foot. Tuck your head down.

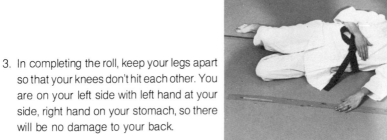

3. In completing the roll, keep your legs apart so that your knees don't hit each other. You are on your left side with left hand at your side, right hand on your stomach, so there will be no damage to your back.

SIDE BREAKFALL

1. Kick your right foot out toward the left front.

2. Proceed to fall to your right side.

3. As you fall to your right side, your right arm hits the ground next to you, with your left hand on your stomach.

AIR ROLL

1. As your right hand comes around in a whipping motion, step forward with your right foot.

2. As you swing your right hand down and around, your left leg is whipping straight up toward the ceiling. Your body will now turn in the air.

3. In completing the fall, land on your right side, with your left hand out and your right hand on your stomach, as in the forward breakfall.

FORWARD BACK BRIDGE
FROM GROUND

1. Put both fists down on the ground, with your right foot coming forward.

2. As you push off with your right foot, both feet will come over the front of your body.

3. Land on the balls of your feet; your arms are at your sides to absorb the shock of your body weight. Your body, except for your feet and shoulder blades, is suspended in the air.

FORWARD FACE FALL

1. Place your hands in front of you, your feet about shoulder-width apart.

2. Now kick your feet out from underneath you, with your hands in front, so they are ready for the point of impact.

3. Turn your head to the left side as your forearms and hands strike the mat. Your body should be suspended in the air with the balls of your feet and your forearms holding you up. Your elbows do not hit the mat.

Attack: Bear Hug from Behind

1. Using your right hand, strike with the knuckles of your index and middle fingers directly to the top of your attacker's hand.

2. With the same knuckles of your left hand, apply the same technique to the top of his hand.

3. Drive your right heel backward onto your attacker's right kneecap.

4. With the right foot still raised, slide down his right shin with your heel and stamp on the instep of his foot.

5. Now drive back with your left foot to your attacker's left kneecap.

6. Again slide down his left shin with your left heel and stamp on his instep.

7. Move your head to the left slightly and strike to your attacker's nose with a right-handed backfist.

8. Move your head to the right side and strike to his nose with a left-handed backfist.

9. Shift your body to the left and swing your right hand down in a hammerfist to your attacker's groin.

10. Shift to your right side and swing your left hand down in a hammerfist to his groin.

Attack: Bear Hug from Front

1. Using two hands, strike with the palms of the hands to your attacker's ears.

2. Strike open-handed with both hands, using the thumb edge of the hands to the side of the neck (carotid artery).

3. Raise your right leg and drive the sole of your foot into your attacker's left knee.

4. Slide down his left shin and strike to his instep with your right heel.

5. Raise your left leg and drive the sole of your foot into your attacker's right knee.

6. Slide down his right shin and strike to his instep with your left heel.

7. Raise your right knee and strike to your attacker's groin.

8. Raise your left knee and strike to your attacker's groin.

9. Right-handed clawhand strike with thumb up under your attacker's nose.

10. Left-handed clawhand strike with thumb up under your attacker's nose.

2

Strikes Against
Vulnerable Areas

In this chapter, we will deal with the natural weapons of your body—hands, feet, elbows, and knees—and with the vulnerable target areas of your attacker's body. Neither the size of these natural weapons nor your own physical strength is the major factor in immobilizing an attacker; it is, rather, the precise timing and delivery of a strike to a vital area. But what about the amount of force needed to stop an attacker? If you are attacked, you must strike as hard and as fast as you can, for the attacker is out to hurt you. But remember that it is your *form* and *speed* which are the major sources of the force you have available. With practice, you will soon realize that you have sufficient force to defend yourself and to immobilize an attacker if you have to. The techniques you are acquiring are designed specifically to maximize the force delivered by a strike; the target areas you will become familiar with are all highly vulnerable. In the illustrations which follow, you will see which blows are likely to be most effective against the various vulnerable target areas on your attacker, from his eyes to his feet. First, however, let us review what damage you can do with a well-aimed hand, foot, elbow, or knee.

You can counterattack easily many areas above your attacker's shoulders. The eyes, ears, nose, temples, forehead, and neck—all are very vulnerable. Any blow to these areas will cause great pain and may well disable an attacker. A strike to the eyes can easily cause temporary or permanent blindness. A blow to the nose can knock a man out; at the least it will cause his eyes to water uncontrollably. A cupped-hand strike to the ears can rupture the eardrum or fracture the jaw; it could knock a man out. If you miss the ears and hit the jaw hinge or the temples, or if you aim for the temples, the blow can still be effective. A blow to the forehead can fracture the skull or the frontal sinus and cause either a slight or a major concussion. Aim for the front or side of the throat and you can damage any of the organs located there. If you strike your attacker at the back of the neck, you can cause whiplash or a broken neck. A hard hit on the top of a vertebra or spinal disc can cause paralysis anywhere below the blow. Do not worry about what you may do to the attacker; remember what he is trying to do to you and remember that he will do it if you don't stop him first.

The trunk of the body provides larger and more readily available targets. Just a moderate blow to the rib cage can break some ribs. If ribs are broken, at the very least your attacker will have trouble breathing and you will gain time to continue your counterattack or to escape. A hard blow to the collarbone can fracture it, paralyzing part or all of the arm on that side. Below the rib cage, you can attack the diaphragm, solar plexus, kidneys, spleen, bladder, and groin. Striking in the diaphragm—the solar plexus region, just below the frontal rib cage—can knock the wind out of an attacker, leaving him at your mercy. It might knock him out or rupture an internal organ, such as the stomach, gall bladder, or pancreas; it might collapse a lung. Any such injury could send your attacker into shock. Blows to the kidneys, to the spleen on the left side of the abdomen, to the bladder, and to the groin might cause internal bleeding, leading to nausea, pain, and/or dizziness.

Your attacker's limbs are vulnerable also. A broken elbow or knee-cap is extremely painful and immobilizing. A hard blow on the shin or foot can splinter the bone and temporarily stop your attacker. Any of the wristlocks shown in chapter 1 can be used to break the wrist or to cause extreme pain. Remember that after any blow to a limb, even an effective one, you will have to follow up with another strike and possibly another.

Study and learn the strikes and targets in this chapter and put them together into patterns of continuous movement. Each blow is not just a blow in self-defense, it is, as well, a step toward the next blow. You must be prepared to fight until you are out of danger.

1. Striking the eyes with fingertips

This strike is usually made with your feet far apart and one leg slightly in front of the other. Grab a body part, such as the arm, if you can, and pull your attacker forward as you strike.

2. Striking under the nose with (1) palmhand or (2) knife-edge

With your feet shoulder-width apart and your right leg slightly in front of you, move toward your attacker and strike into his nose, driving him backward.

3. Striking the front or side of the throat with (1) clawhand, (2) knife-edge, or (3) inside knife-edge

Put your right leg forward and strike your attacker in his throat. If you can grab your attacker, pull him toward you at the same time.

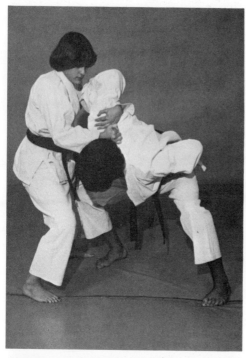

4. Striking the back of the neck with (1) hammerfist or (2) downward elbow strike

If your attacker is bent over, strike down, at the same time squatting down with him. If you need to, you can also drive his face into your knee.

5. Striking the temple with (1) elbow or (2) backfist

In these movements, a wristlock is applied with the elbow. Step forward and drive your other elbow into your attacker's temple or strike it with a backfist. Your feet should be apart in a balanced stance at the end of either strike.

6. Striking the bridge of the nose with (1) forehand or (2) backfist

Step in with your right foot and pull your attacker's wrist toward you as you strike.

7. Striking the ears with cupped hands

This strike is useful when your attacker has you immobile, but your hands are free. Strike the tops of his ears with the palms of both hands as hard as you can.

8. Striking the jawbone with (1) elbow, (2) palmhand, or (3) knee

Strike upward as you step forward and pull your attacker toward you by the wrist.

9. Striking the center of the forehead with (1) elbow or (2) knee

As you strike with your elbow, try to grab your attacker's head with your opposite hand and pull his head into the blow.

As you drive your knee up into your attacker's head push down on the back of his head with your hand. This can be done from the armbar lock, as illustrated.

10. Striking the spinal column with elbow

With your attacker bent forward, squat and drive your elbow straight down onto his spinal column.

11. Striking the rib cage with (1) elbow, (2) fist, or (3) foot

With your feet shoulder-width apart, try to put your attacker in an outstretched position by pulling on his wrist as you make the strike.

12. Striking the solar plexus with (1) elbow, (2) foot, or (3) knee

With the elbow and foot strikes, pull your attacker off balance and move forward with your strike.

With the knee strike, pull his upper body down as you meet his midsection with your knee.

13. Striking the kidney with (1) elbow or (2) punch

You should be slightly to the rear of your attacker, with your feet shoulder-width apart. Move toward your attacker as you strike.

14. Striking the spleen with (1) foot or (2) fist

When striking with the foot, always be sure to keep your balance and move toward your attacker.

With the fist strike, keep one foot ahead of the other to get maximum power.

15. Striking the bladder with (1) reverse hammerfist or (2) elbow

    With the hammerfist strike, you must be low with your feet wide apart; strike in an upward motion.

    When you strike with the elbow to this area, drop to one knee and strike directly up. With both strikes, remember to keep your attacker outstretched by pulling out on his wrist.

16. Striking the diaphragm with (1) elbow or (2) hammerfist

Keep one leg forward and the other back for strength and balance. Attempt to grab the back of your attacker's head and bring him forward into the strike.

17. Striking the collarbone with (1) elbow or (2) hammerfist

Keep your feet apart in the horse rider's stance and strike straight down on top of your attacker's collarbone.

18. Striking and breaking the elbow with (1) forearm and outside wristlock or (2) armbar lock

With your attacker's wrist in an outside lock, pivot to that side so that one leg is in front of the other and drive your forearm directly into your attacker's elbow.

To use an armbar lock, catch your attacker's arm over your shoulder so that his elbow is locked and pull toward yourself with both hands.

19. Striking the groin with (1) palmhand, (2) ball or instep of foot, or (3) knee

    Step forward and drive your palm up into your attacker's groin.

    To use your foot, grab your attacker and pull him toward you as you drive your foot into his groin.

    Use the knee when you are close to your attacker, for example, in a bear hug; just drive your knee up.

20. Striking the shin with (1) side kick or (2) heel of shoe

Hold on to your attacker so he cannot back away from the blow and simply drive either strike back into the shin.

21. Striking the back of the knee with (1) blade of foot or (2) heel kick

You should be behind your attacker, pulling him toward you by the hair or the collar. Aim both strikes directly into the back of his knee.

22. Striking the front of the knee with (1) side kick or (2) heel kick

Hold on to your attacker and pull him toward you as you drive your foot at his knee.

3

Attack and Counterattack

Rape can occur anywhere at any time. A rapist does not care where or when he attacks. In an environment in which there are many people about, he may approach you nonviolently at first and then threaten you if you do not respond favorably. Perhaps he will pinch your neck or twist your arm. The majority of rapes, however, take place in secluded areas, where no help is handy. They are violent, aggressive, brutal, and sometimes fatal.

If you are to defend yourself, you must learn, first of all, to overcome fear and panic. You must be ready to act quickly with a succession of blocks, strikes, and evasions. The more you practice the basic techniques and strikes presented in the first two chapters, the more confident you will become in your own power and in your ability to defend yourself. You will be ready to counterattack spontaneously. Balance, speed, and control will be built into your reactions.

In the following pages, a number of possible attacks are pictured, as well as suggested defenses. Use these as the bases for your practice exercises and remember that you should be able to move either left or right. Practice each defense to both sides. When you feel confident in the moves pictured here, invent variations of your own and responses to other conceivable attacks.

At the end of the chapter, a number of situations are shown with more than one assailant. If you are faced with such a situation, you

54 must use your judgment. If you can disable one attacker quickly, you stand a good chance of scaring off the rest. Survey the area for any possible weapons—sticks, stones, etc. When you counterattack the first assailant, try to use his body as a shield; use an armlock or a grab to the carotid artery. One final reminder—do not forget your shout. It increases the force of your strike and it will confuse your attacker.

Attack 1

1. You are being attacked from the front in a crosshand choke (one hand over the other grabbing your lapel). Your attacker applies pressure by raising his elbows and pulling you forward.

2. As your attacker pulls you inward toward him, raise your right knee and strike to his groin.

3. You then strike to his floating (lower) ribs with both hands, using the thumb edge of hand.

4. Place both hands on your attacker's neck and push him backward as you hook his left leg with your right leg.

Attack 2

1. Your attacker grabs you from behind in a right-arm choke, with his forearm applying pressure to the center of your throat.

2. Stamp down hard on instep of your attacker's foot with your heel.

3. Pivot to your left and strike to his rib cage with your left elbow.

4. Now turn back to the right and grab your attacker's hair with your right hand and his elbow with your left hand.

5. Bend your right knee and pull your attacker directly over your right shoulder.

Attack 3

1. Your attacker grabs you from behind in a two-handed choke around the neck, with his fingertips meeting in the front.

2. While maintaining your balance, bring either your right or left knee up and drive your foot backward to your attacker's kneecap, or to his groin if possible.

3. Complete the movement by grabbing your own right wrist with your left hand and ramming your right elbow into his midsection or groin.

Attack 4

1. Your attacker has grabbed you from behind in a full nelson and is raising you slightly off the ground.

2. As he raises you up, bring both legs up in the air and then drive them backward, hitting him on the knees or shins.

3. While your attacker is still bent forward, drive your head back, striking with the back of your head to the bridge of his nose.

Attack 5

1. Your attacker has grabbed you from behind in a right-arm choke with his left hand over your mouth and is slowly dragging you backward.

2. Stamp down hard with your heel on the instep of your attacker's foot.

3. Quickly bend forward at the waist, driving your hips into his groin. This movement will bend your attacker forward.

4. While in this position, drive the back of your head into your attacker's face, hitting the bridge of his nose if possible.

5. If necessary, step to one side and strike with a hard backfist to his face.

Attack 6

1. Your attacker has grabbed you from behind in a left-arm choke, with his right hand grabbing your hair and pulling back on it.

2. Make your left hand into a fist and place this on top of your attacker's right hand.

3. Now bring your right hand up on top of your left hand and apply pressure downward so that the knuckles of your left hand are pressing into your attacker's hand. This will at least cause him to loosen his grip.

4. Your left hand now grabs his right wrist while your right elbow strikes to his solar plexus.

5. Immediately grab your attacker's right elbow and drive it upward, breaking his arm.

Attack 7

1. Your attacker is grabbing you from the front in a choke, with both hands meeting behind your neck.

2. Immediately kick to your attacker's knee or shin to loosen him up.

3. With both hands open, strike with the heels of your hands to his ears.

4. Grab his ears and pull back and downward, throwing him to the ground.

Attack 8

1. Your attacker has his left hand around your neck (cutting off your wind), while his right hand is raised to strike you in the face.

2. Block his right-handed strike with your left forearm.

 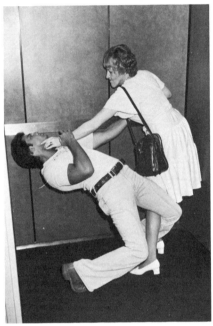

3. Immediately grab your attacker's left hand with your right hand in an outside wristlock.

4. At the same time, strike at his neck with your left hand. Drop him to the ground, hooking his left leg if necessary.

Attack 9

1. Your attacker has grabbed you from behind with his right hand around your throat and is slowly pulling you backward with his left hand on your hair.

2. Pivot to the right and drive your right elbow deep into your attacker's rib cage or midsection, thus causing him to bend forward.

3. As he does so, bring your left hand up and strike with the heel of the hand to either the nose or the chin and drive him backward to the ground.

Attack 10

1. Your attacker has you held against a wall with his left forearm against your throat and his right hand on your blouse (as though to rip it off).

2. With both hands open, strike to your attacker's ears with the palms of your hands. At the same time, strike to his groin with your knee.

3. Place your thumbs under his nose and drive backward and down until he drops.

4. Once he is down, you may strike to any part of his body with your heel.

1. You have both of your hands up in front of you as if to push your attacker away, and he has grabbed your hands by the wrists with both of his hands.

2. As your attacker grabs your wrists, let him pull you inward toward him. While he is doing this, you immediately strike hard with your right knee or right foot to his groin.

4. You then have the power to drive your attacker backward; proceed to hook his inner leg and push back, throwing him to the ground.

3. Snap your hands away and toward your attacker's face, with both thumbs landing directly under his nose.

Attack 12

1. Your attacker is grabbing you from the front in a tightly gripped waist hold, and is attempting to kiss you on the lips.

2. Without panic, you go directly into action by striking with your left hand to your attacker's neck and grabbing his groin.

3. As you are going into both grabs, you should turn slightly to your left so you will be in a better position to push down on your attacker's neck and pull on his groin.

4. With this, simply move back to give yourself more pulling power upward on his groin.

1. Your attacker has both your shoulders pinned against the wall, with his hands on your shoulders.

2. As your attacker is leaning on your shoulders with both of his arms, you immediately strike in a circular outward motion, with your forearms to your attacker's inner arms.

3. Your attacker should then fall slightly forward toward you; as he does this, quickly strike with both of your hands to the sides of his neck.

4. To complete the movement, you will grab his head firmly and drive it downward, facefirst to either one of your knees.

Attack 14

1. Your attacker grabs your lapels with both of his hands and begins to rough you up.

2. As your attacker has a grip on your lapels with both of his hands, you should immediately grab his right hand with your right hand in an outside wristlock and twist to your right side.

3. As you are twisting your attacker's hand to the right side, quickly strike with your left elbow to his face or the side of his head (temple).

4. To complete the movement, take your elbow, which has just struck your attacker in the face, and snap it back to your rear; now hit your attacker in the nose and land him on the ground.

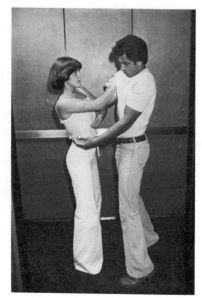

1. Your attacker has his right hand moving behind you, as his left hand is on top of your right shoulder.

2. You take action by bringing your left arm over and around, then moving it directly upward on your attacker's elbow.

4. In completing the movement, you should step in with your left leg and immediately sweep down and back with your right leg, dropping him to the ground.

3. You then strike with an open hand to your attacker's throat.

Attack 16

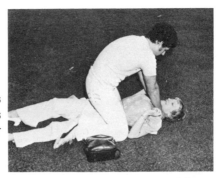

1. Your attacker has you on the ground and is straddling you; at the same time, he is choking you with both hands around your neck.

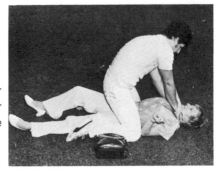

2. You quickly reach across the front of your body with your right hand and grab your attacker's hand at the wrist in an outside wristlock.

3. Quickly turn his hand to your right side and simultaneously strike with your left forearm to his right elbow.

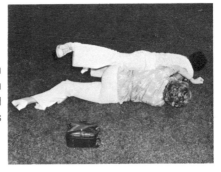

4. To help complete this movement, as you are turning and striking to the elbow, you simply turn your body to the right side and lift your left knee directly into his groin, thus moving him completely off of you.

Attack 17

1. Your attacker has both of your hands down on the ground and is holding them by the wrists; he is also straddling your body and attempting to kiss you on the mouth.

2. With as much power as you have, you should try to slide your hands directly above your head. You are simultaneously striking very hard with your knees to your attacker's buttocks to knock him off balance.

3. As you do this, you strike directly to his face with your forehead.

4. To complete this movement, you should face your attacker, go to the left or right side of your body, and strike with the opposite hand to his neck.

Attack 18

1. You are lying on your back as your attacker is straddling your stomach and covering your mouth (to prevent you from screaming) with his left hand. With his right hand, he is trying to pull off your blouse.

2. While both your hands are free, you grab your attacker's hair with your left hand and pull him to your left side.

3. As you start to move him toward the left, quickly strike with your right hand to the side of his neck with a hard fingertip strike.

4. Without releasing any pressure on his throat or hair, you then pull your attacker down to your left side. Raise your right hand up and strike directly down on top of his groin.

1. Your attacker is grabbing both of your wrists with his hands, or grabbing for your sleeves.

2. In a quick circular motion, turn both of your hands to the outside, with your palms facing your attacker. You then grab both of his wrists with your hands and snap a front kick to his groin as you pull him inward.

3. As your attacker bends over from the force of the kick, you immediately grab his head from behind and snap it downward, so that his face meets your right knee.

4. In order to rid yourself completely of your attacker, grab his hair and sweep out his left leg with your right leg, directly dropping him to the ground.

Attack 20

1. Your attacker has you pinned against the wall with both of your hands in an upward position; his body is now very close to yours.

2. Your movement is limited in a position such as this, so you must react very quickly. Strike with your right knee to your attacker's groin.

3. Strike straight downward onto your attacker's foot with the heel of your right foot.

4. To complete the movement, you hook the inside of your attacker's leg and strike to his nose with a palmhand, driving him directly backward to the ground.

Attack 21

1. Your attacker has your head against the wall, with his left hand pulling back on your hair. He is now about to strike you with his right hand directly across the face.

2. Your arms are free, and you immediately block your attacker's strike with a left forearm block.

3. As you are blocking, you make a hard fingertip strike to his eyes with your right hand.

4. You now drive your left elbow directly into your attacker's rib cage.

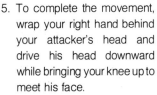

5. To complete the movement, wrap your right hand behind your attacker's head and drive his head downward while bringing your knee up to meet his face.

1. Your attacker is pinning you against the wall with his belt pushed up against your throat. He has the belt gripped in both hands.

2. From this position, you act quickly by striking your attacker's ears with the palms of your hands.

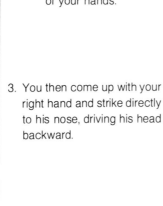

3. You then come up with your right hand and strike directly to his nose, driving his head backward.

4. While driving his nose backward, you reach down with your left hand and grab his groin.

5. Continue the movement by pulling up on his groin and driving back on his nose. This will complete your movement.

1. As you are sitting behind your desk, your attacker reaches over your desk with his right hand and starts to pull down the top of your blouse.

2. Put your right hand directly on top of your attacker's hand (as if to make him think you are going along with him).

3. Reach over in a downward wristlock and snap his hand directly down as hard as you can, using your other hand for extra power.

4. With your attacker now facedown on your desk, you then strike straight down with a hammerfist to the back of his neck, if necessary.

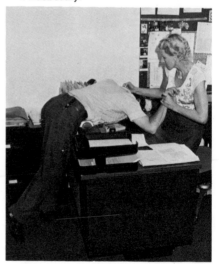

1. Your attacker has stepped behind your desk and is proceeding to caress your neck while you are seated.

2. With your attacker standing very close to you, you take the elbow closest to him and ram it directly into his midsection or groin.

3. As he bends forward in pain, you immediately turn and strike with your opposite hand directly upward to your attacker's throat, driving him back.

4. This will complete the movement, as you cause him to fall backward.

1. Your attacker is placing his right arm around your shoulders and his left hand on top of your lap.

2. Without panic, you pretend to go along with your attacker and put your left arm over his shoulders.

3. You now drop your arm down and lock it as hard as you can on your attacker's elbow.

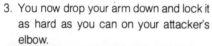

4. You now step outward and immediately strike to his groin with your right hand.

5. Without letting go of your attacker, you sit directly to your right side and throw him over.

6. As he is thrown over, you hang on to him, using his body weight to pull you over on top of him.

7. To complete the movement, as you are straddled across his stomach, keep the elbow lock and strike directly down with your right hand to his throat.

1. You are sitting on a park bench with your attacker on your left. He places his right hand directly on your inner thigh. Calmly, you place your left hand on top of your attacker's (as if to go along with him).

2. As your hand goes into an inside wrist-lock, you immediately step outward with your right foot, simultaneously holding tight on your wristlock.

4. To complete the movement, you drop back onto your left knee and throw your attacker to the ground, breaking his wrist, which you hold with both of your hands.

3. You then strike to his eyes with the right index finger and middle finger.

Attack 27

1. As you are sitting on a park bench, your attacker places his right arm around your shoulders and proceeds to hold you close to him.

2. As you put your left arm around your attacker's shoulders, as if to go along with him, you will then drop your arm straight down and around to his right elbow, driving it straight up.

3. You now stand up, turning to face him, and strike with your right hand to your attacker's throat.

4. In completing the movement, you pull his elbow toward you and strike with your right knee to his groin.

Attack 28

1. Your first attacker is grabbing you from behind with his hands tightly around your wrists. As he is doing this, your second attacker lunges forward in front of you as if to choke you.

2. With this, you snap out a forward heel kick to your second attacker's groin or kneecap.

3. As your foot comes back down to the ground, you squat down low and move your left foot behind your first attacker's right leg.

4. While doing this, take your right hand and swing it to your left hand, grabbing your first attacker's right wrist with your left hand.

5. Witn your first attacker's body bent forward and his wrists grabbed in a downward motion, you then strike with your right hand to the back of his neck with a knife edge.

6. To complete the movement, you grab his hair and pull back as you simultaneously strike with your right knee to his face.

1. As your first attacker has you grabbed around the waist from behind, your second attacker is in front of you grabbing both sides of your face.

2. You immediately react by attacking your front attacker with the palms of both of your hands directly on top of his ears.

3. Immediately pull his head downward toward your right knee, which you lift up.

4. Coming down with your foot, you then strike with your heel directly onto your rear attacker's instep (either one of his feet).

5. You then take your right elbow and swing it directly around to his temple with great force.

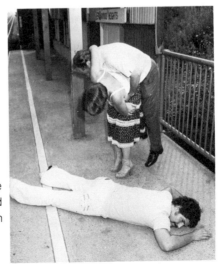

6. In completing the movement, you take your right arm and wrap it directly around his head as you drop forward, throwing him over your hip.

Attack 30

1. One of your attackers is covering your mouth from behind with his left hand as his right forearm is choking you around the neck.

2. You immediately strike with your left elbow directly into his diaphragm.

3. You then reach up with both hands to your right side and grab his hair, throwing him directly down as you drop to your right knee.

4. Your next attacker is now grabbing you by the hair with his right hand while you are still on your knee.

5. As he proceeds to pick you up by your hair, you then grab his right hand with your left and step back into him, striking with a straight elbow strike to the groin. This should complete the movement.

Attack 31

1. Your first attacker is coming from behind with a belt and starts to choke you by wrapping it around your neck.

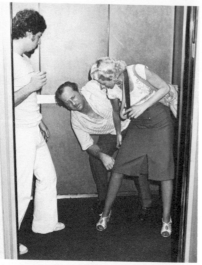

2. As you are being choked, you immediately shift your hip to your left side and strike with your right hand to your attacker's groin.

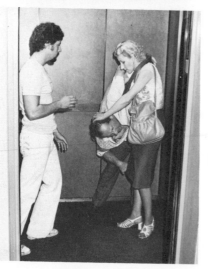

3. As you finish the strike, you bring your right hand up and around in a counterclockwise motion around your attacker's head.

4. While your arm is around your attacker's head, you drive his head downward so that his face meets your left knee.

5. Your next attacker is grabbing you around the neck and pushing you hard against the wall.

6. You now grab his right hand in a wristlock with your left hand, as you simultaneously strike with your right foot to his shin.

7. In completing the movement, you drive your right-hand index and middle fingers into his eyes.

Attack 32

1. Your first attacker is choking you from behind in a right forearm choke. You immediately drive your right foot straight back on top of his kneecap.

2. As he releases you, lean to your left side and drive your left elbow directly into his diaphragm.

3. Your other attacker is now grabbing you around the front of your throat with both of his hands.

4. As he is doing this, you strike directly down to the crook of his arm with your left forearm.

5. Follow this with an open-handed strike directly up and into his nose. This should complete your movement.

4

Pocketbook Weapons, Canes, and Umbrellas

No one is allowed to carry a concealed weapon. It is not against the law, however, to carry such personal articles as keys, a hairbrush, a comb, or a pen. Nor is it illegal to carry a cane or an umbrella. Any of these articles make effective weapons, and you should work them into your practice routines.

In this chapter, counterattacks using pocketbook items, canes, and umbrellas are shown. Remember that you must have such weapons within easy reach if they are to be of any use to you. Don't bury your keys in your pocketbook; carry them in your pocket and put another pocketbook item in your other pocket.

Effective Strikes

1. Strike with the umbrella tip to the side of your attacker's throat under the jaw to the carotid artery. For maximum effect in this movement, your feet should be separated and you should strike with a forward thrust.

2. Strike to your attacker's temple with the side of the cane.

3. Strike to your attacker's rib cage in a forward-lunging umbrella-tip strike. This strike is very effective when you are being grabbed in a two-handed choke from the front.

4. With your attacker holding you in a bear hug from the front, grab your umbrella quickly with both hands a shoulder-width apart and hold the umbrella in front of you. Then strike upward to the bottom of your attacker's nose, bringing him backward.

5. Strike to the bottom of your attacker's nose, driving your umbrella backward with both hands.

6. A forward-moving strike to your attacker's diaphragm (below the lower ribs) with the end of a cane.

7. Strike to your attacker's armpit. Strike in an upward motion with the end of your umbrella, as if to lift your attacker directly up onto his toes.

8. Your attacker is grabbing you in a forward choke with both of his hands firmly around your neck. With your keys, strike directly to your attacker's eye sockets.

9. With a hairbrush, strike directly to your attacker's Adam's apple, holding either end of the hairbrush.

10. Using a pen or pencil, you again aim for the eyes, but this time, drive your weapon directly into the eye.

11. With a comb, preferably a metal one, strike directly upward from your attacker's chin to his forehead or nose.

12. With your keys, strike directly up-
    ward under your attacker's nose or
    strike directly onto the bridge of his
    nose.

13. Using either end of your hairbrush,
    strike to your attacker's temple.

14. As you hold one side of your attacker's head with your hand, take your pen and drive it directly into the side of his neck (carotid artery).

15. Taking your comb, strike directly under your attacker's neck in an upward motion. With this movement, you should be able to drive him backward.

1. Your attacker has his hands gripped firmly around your neck and is choking you. Quickly drive the umbrella tip directly into your attacker's diaphragm.

2. Snap the other end of the umbrella around and straight into your attacker's face.

3. To complete the movement, continue your umbrella strike to the face in a downward motion.

Attack 2

1. Your attacker has grabbed you by the lapel with his right hand and is proceeding to draw you to him.

2. As your cane is in your right hand, you simply bring it across and in front of you, grabbing it with your left hand, palm down.

3. With the cane gripped firmly with both hands, strike straight down on top of your attacker's wrist or knuckles.

4. To complete the movement, take the cane and drive it directly upward to his throat. This should easily complete your defense.

Attack 3

1. As you are walking, your attacker on your left is placing his right arm around your shoulder and slowly forcing you to walk where he wants. With your umbrella in your right hand, simply pivot with both feet toward your attacker.

2. While turning, bring your umbrella up into your other hand and drive it deep into his midsection.

3. As your attacker is bent over in pain, take your right hand with the end of your umbrella and strike up into his face.

4. While striking to the facial area, step with your right foot behind your attacker and drive him straight down to the ground.

Attack 4

1. Your attacker has you firmly around the waist in a bear hug; as he applies pressure, you must act quickly by stamping with your heel to the instep of his foot.

2. Snap your right hand with your cane in an upward motion to the back of his head.

3. As you have struck your attacker to the back of his head, then grab the cane with your other hand and bring it down on the back of your attacker's neck. Keep constant pressure directly on his neck, which should be on your shoulder.

4. Drop to your right knee and pull your attacker down with direct pressure to the back of the neck.

Attack 5

1. Your attacker is holding you firmly around the waist and your cane is in your right hand. Quickly snap the cane across to your left hand.

2. Strike with a rolling motion to your attacker's lower back. Your attacker is in pain and should release you.

3. Immediately bring your cane up and around to the front of his throat. You then complete the movement by hooking your attacker's left leg with your right leg, throwing him directly down with the cane pushing on his throat.

Attack 6

1. Your attacker has your hair in his left hand and is pulling you back; as he does this, he also has his right hand over your mouth. Quickly step back and snap your cane down onto your attacker's left hand.

2. Drop your cane down to your waist and, as you pivot on your right foot, drive the cane directly into your attacker's midsection.

3. Bring your cane around in a clockwise motion and snap it into his neck.